BODY SPELLS

ZERO

For anyone who has ever battled with their body. May we never win.

CONTENTS

PREFACE

These poems, presented (mostly) chronologically, were written between 2018 and 2022. In that time, things happened. They always do.

I

CIRCA SENIOR YEAR OF HIGH SCHOOL, 2018

YOU TAKE ME OUT

Okay, so I know it's desperation sinking in, not any genuine sort of pull. Does that make my breathing any less painful? Really? Tears cool my contacts and slip down to salt my cheeks. I have no idea why I'm sitting here, waiting like this.

I have a book. I could read. I still have some time left of my youth to be that pretty intellectual with her book and coffee, waiting for the approach. They're too cool for what I am, though, and my dark thoughts and twists are actually a genuine malignance, not some act. I am actually sick.

Because I want women. Fuck—I like women, not men. This could be a problem if one ever likes me back. So far, so good.

I guess.

Men I could maybe stand. Men I can tolerate. Men, too, are easier. But, worth it? I don't know. Their company—none of it—can make up for the debasement. I can't see any point to it.

I think my finger is about to rot off. I think that mole gets darker every day and I debate whether or not it counts as a suicide to just ignore it. I think, I wait, I sit. Not much else left to do for a fat-faced hysteric.

Walk by, say hi. I'm all that's left of me.

GIRL NO.2

It's always a he in these things, yeah?
Well, mine was actually a she,
the girl-daemon who tried to eat
at my ankles once or twice.

I guess you could say we were in love—
tangled up in the swing set,
stripped down to our underwear on a February
black,
we smoked pot out of soda cans until the world
would stop
spinning.

But she loved boys,
and I really mean she loved the hump
and heave of their weight on top.
She couldn't help but pout those purpled lips
while she slipped
another ring in her ear,
Real baby-princess bullshit stuff that brought the
creeps in droves.

She would beg me to braid out that long blond
mess though—
I did like slowly working my hands
through the tangles and turning it
into a Celtic rope streaming down her back.

She'd always flip it onto her shoulder to pet it, the
truest
animal of her affections,
herself.

II

CIRCA MY 1.5 SEMESTERS IN COMMUNITY COLLEGE, 2018

"YOU CAN BE A REAL BITCH SOMETIMES."

She was a honey pie and a half until she decided to turn around on me. I stood amazed for nearly a year, trying to connect that the blonde who planted Coral Matte kisses on my cheek also put the weepy rip in my chest.

SEMI-SESTINAS FOR THE TRAGIC LOVE AFFAIR

The Meeting Sestina

I must say, you are extraordinary.

Extraordinary! I must—You are.

I?

Extraordinary, you say?

You say you must? I say, I must.

You, I, extraordinary.

The Romance Sestina

We have fire they'll never understand.

They'll never have fire.

We understand fire. They'll never.

They'll never have *we*.

We have *we*; we never have *we never*.

We'll never.

The Grief Sestina

My God, why is she gone?

My She, gone.

Why?

She is gone.

She is my God. God is gone.

Why is God gone?

The Killing Sestina

I must say, you are extraordinary.
We have fire they'll never understand.
My God, why is she gone?

You never understand God.

My God is extraordinary.

They'll never have, never understand my God.

My God is fire.

Extraordinary!

She is you—you understand?

You are my God.

God—why you fire, gone?

I never understand "gone."

I never understand

God gone,

fire gone,

we gone.

I'll never understand.

You say I must—I'll never.

ROMANCE GAGGER

Maddening love—that sickening thing.
Affliction's got your best girls
(The very very best of them.)
reduced to blackened lashes and
(Oh God, the very best!)
heart palpitations and
3 am calls crying over a text left on read.
You nurse each one back to heart just in time
for the next great break.

You've known that love is but a coupling,
you guess,
and fucking is just fucking,
but their glossed-up mouths running on about

making love

and that god damn idea of

electric sparks and *Romeo at last*

has got you so far and away you're stuck

in this echoing dorm wondering, really,

if maybe you're just some bitter bitch

(who would need to know to know).

And, yes, okay—

"you" isn't you, it's me.

Cuz I don't fucking know you, anyhow.

I'm the bitter bitch that sits against an undecorated wall
when dinner is over.

Bitter bitch to wear and hang like shirt sleeves.

Let me hurt vicariously through you.

Please.

WALL, CURTAIN, THEN MASK

It's a funny exchange that I've lured y'all into—
You watch a stranger with her back turned
slipping secrets thrown in words,
I get little hills of data that almost ease an
eager ego.

I talk about nothing, really.
Talk about my dorm and my feelings and
how I hide my Self.
There's a few things I could bare that'd get me clicks—
like necrotic flesh and fake intimacies and fantastic sorrows
that'd get you calling me an Interesting Girl.
I could do it.

But I'm not like that.
I'm not gonna give away whatever people want
and get left with nothing.
I got barriers built for a reason.
Keep someone at length and they'll fall in love.

And maybe I want y'all to love me.
I mean, everybody does—
wanna get loved by the world.
So maybe I'm a little more of a person than I'm trying
to let on.

Here's the deal, then:
If you decide to go ahead and give me the adore,
to go ahead and make me Digitally Beloved,
then I can do this—

Crumb by crumb makes the cake.
Brick by brick tears down the wall.
I'll offer out strips of my soul
(for everyone but also only for you)
and then

perhaps

something past my megalomania.

A DARLING'S DILEMMA

Baby!, you're gonna kill me for this.

Not that you wouldn't anyways—we've fathered a few beautiful crime scenes together:

1. Me made like Old Hollywood, shot classy in that Vegas love suite you sprung for.
2. Me in the one-piece, throat slashed in the Daytona low tide.
3. Me just home from work, surprised by a charger cord in the living room.
4. Me a full mess, cut to bits across that rose garden (you've always had an eye for the ironic).

So I guess let's see if you can top it with this *one.*

Cheating isn't the right word for it, but how can I resist every other wolf in the world? It's unfair for you to expect me intact all the way into the evenings.

And I've tried to quit "posing like a Dahlia," as you put it, but it's not snap-simple like you think.

I tried kissing your flaws to couplets, but all I got was kindling.

So do me how you will, honey.
Because you always will, honey.
Even when my lines go limp and my face grows funny—
honey.
I'm not one to be made but of blood and money—
honey.
Listen, please,
because I know there's not too much left of me.
I traded my eyes and mouth for a you called He.
And worship, fast, for I knew you'd never else give me
free.

You've taught me to be everyone's little victim.

I'VE GOT 10X10 FOOTSTEPS IN THIS LAND AND I'LL TRADE YOU HAPPILY

I can speak
out loud
without need.
I should feel free,
like bird off land and fish in sea,
and yet I find myself without *want* to speak.

I can stay right between these walls.
Forever. Really.
I have never feared what's held in here.
Those noises stay just in those halls.
No eyes can scan past my plane so tall,
No hands can chase to squeeze me raw.

I am safe.

And not safe like sound

but safe like bound,

and bound like glued to the floor,

like nobody could ever again pull me past that door.

I don't care to fall back for a lover,

can't truly seek within them a secure cover.

I hear men grow fickle after phallus introduced,

and I desire a shelter tight, not loose.

So, door is door and lock is lock,

and my body stays as unmoved as rock.

Yes, flesh remains unloved,

but here to love means simply to corrupt.

And if I grow past my ceiling?

If I really grasp further than my reaching?

Easy.

I'll simply stoop until I'm again smaller,

and starve myself so I get no taller.

This is the life I have to claim,

a day-by-day that goes all the same.

It's not bad this way—there's none of that weeping.

It's peace and quiet, if I just ignore the mind

screeching.

THE ROOM IS ALL MINE AND EMPTY TONIGHT.

I press fingers onto keys, yet I make no music.

— A LINE I THOUGHT WAS PAINFULLY CLEVER.

Of course I'm depressed. Surrounded by pierced bullets and broadcasted agonies, of course I'm depressed. Of course I think I'm the worst that ever was. Ignore Sylvia and those who puts blades on wrist, because they are not me. The world will end with me, and I will end with the earth.

He took a needle to his heart the other day. I seethe over my vice-grip lungs and prickled skin, but he takes those bags and vomit and chairs with that big smile and kisses for everyone. He never cries.

And I weep for the man who never lived to see his acclaim. For those without arms. For the woman with her knees up to her clavicle screaming, "When will this all go away?!" For the juvenile half-cocked by their bedside. Most of all, I shed for myself, the biggest tragedy to ever make it to the dawn.

Eyes of the world. Heart of them all. I run my dreams into the ground. Everything fails in time.

I am vulgar and profane and infinite. I will be multiplied by kin and succumb to a run-down cavity like everyone else. Mortal one, mortals forever.

I'd show you the blank stare up to the ceiling and the rough hands slowly pulling up at the sides of the face, but it's boring. You've seen it before. Fan swirling round and round in the middle of the night. But sometimes clichés say everything I want to.

What the fuck am I doing here? 5-second blinks and a cotton tongue. Fuck that. Fuck you. Fuck everything. And it's all *fuck* and *shit* and *cunt* and *ass* because that's the only way I know how to talk anymore.

Sometimes, vaguely, I can just see a way out. The old hope of doing it draws me back home. Follow, goddamit. And then it is almost there, everything I ever wanted right fucking there, and my fists grope like forever to get it—

and then it's gone. I forget. The taste retreats and fades back. I'm lost again in ads and phone screens and frozen dinners and voices all around in that same indifferent pitch of Whatever.

I press fingers onto keys, and yet I make no music.

PLEASE SOMEONE SAY HI

I just open apps in the elevator.

I'm not actually doing anything but putting my eyes on something other than

people

and I wish I had something that'd actually keep my eyes off all these

people.

Emails and texts back and

Ping! Ding! Yes!

Someone likes me, That!

Play with my keys in the hallway.

Balance a book while I eat.

Gotta lock the door behind me.

Gotta remind myself it's a retreat.

If I'm not in class I'm in my dorm and if I'm not in my chair I'm in my bed and if I'm not asleep

I just really wish I was.

Call home to bleed another lie.

Call home yelling that "I'm fine!"

College was supposed to make me

SOCIAL

and talking about that murder case isn't

SOCIAL

and I'll really need to thin out if I want to be

SOCIAL

and please just let me go to bed now

love you bye.

I'm not, like, crying over this.

Don't think I'm actually s-a-d.

I've always lived in it.

I've always just been me.

The puffy one with the loudest voice.

Pre-k to final grade.

I've been told I've got a way of making myself seem

Unreal.

I'm sorry.

It's not some real choice.

The puffy one.

Puffed up.

Stuffed with thoughts that'd make some freak.

So mortified of my own flesh and mind that I gotta

turn myself out a comedy.

Laughter'll keep others away.

But what's really funny is how the ones who run like cartoons

are the ones who hold the most shame.

Friends could fall in.

Friends are who stop in for a chat,

and I'm the freaking Chat Master.

Whoever can run their mouth—

well, I can run mine faster.

Lovers too...

lovers yet?

Mm.

For me, who?

Who'd match with this mauled head?

But I'll take the part of the Whimsy Girl
if you'll just take the first line
"Oh, hi."
Let's get coffee and practice with our
new empathy ears and
I promise never to linger on a
Aight, bye.

There's still sprinkles that try to say

> *You can do things real.*
> *You can have things permanent.*
> *This isn't how you really feel.*
> *This is just you being lone-sick.*

and I'm getting better at never giving them more than
a couple minutes a day.

Last thing, I promise.
If you happen to catch some eyes—if—
and they're shaded Desperation,
maybe it wouldn't be bad to ask
how their day's been.

Cuz really

past the whole Hate-Myself spiel

I just crave kindness

the way others itch to kill.

Now how does that sound???

WOMAN WORSE

Eve driven out by snake
and Ophelia's to water take.
Thisbe on sword fell,
Antigone swings in her caved Hell.
O Juliet! did poison kiss
and Blanche fixed in delusion's bliss.
Madame Butterfly cut up over man,
Eponine took musket while others ran.
Esmeralda strung for saying no
Lolita doomed from the go.

Sharon stabbed all over paper,
Sylvia's sainted words couldn't save her.
Zelda burnt up before closed eyes,
Marilyn swallowed down an out from all the lies.
Nicole sprawled out under starry steps
and for when other Nikki'd crack, they placed their bets.
Selena already marked for dead as she fled
while at least Amy faded in her own home bed.

Oh there's nothing like a pair of tits

to make a tragedy really stick.
Headlines always sell best
when it's got a dead girl half undressed.
Eyes can't help being caught locked on a corpse
ears prick up when she screams herself hoarse.
We all love woman putting up a show, of course.
And it's always good when she's being done

Woman Worse, Woman Worse.

III

CIRCA WHEN I STARTED GETTING SKINNY, 2019

FAILING MARY (NOTES FROM A VIRGIN)

If I'm pretty, you'll wanna hear it:

> how I can smell skin, the chants pulled from my mouth, what color chips off my shaky fingers.

And if I'm not pretty, it's details for further revulsion. A plain or even an ugly girl must keep at least repression as her virtue. A Belle that likes to get that kind of twisted is forgivable, because the thought of her all twisted up stokes thoughts of getting her twisted up and—

But remember me? When I was big and *sturdy* and gently told that my extras were starting into deformation? People say they saw me then, but that only carries so much weight now (ha!).

What I like about what I like now is that it's all and only about *here* and *right now*. We can play the exact same dance/drama/cliché and it still results like the first findings. Sometimes I even feel almost like a Belle, too. Each encounter leaves me edging a little more closely into grace, into a girl that can *move* and mean it.

I used to think—when I used to think—that I needed that partner as a constant, as a *partner*. But I don't think like that anymore. I'm here for me now, sort of. I'm working on being here for me.

And I guess that makes me some kind of way, huh?

A SWEETIE'S SESTINA (OR, "IF THE WHORE OF BABYLON HAD A MOTHER IN YOUTH")

(I think that the holy Whore had a mother in youth, and I think that that mother drove Her sick to death of being raised into another Sarah or Martha or whatever. She's not the scariest Revelation for the end of the world, really.)

The rules are simple, ya feel?
Where He goes, you follow.
When He's hungry, you feed.
And what He wants, you fill.
Keep to the three and avoid a fight.
What if He really blazes? Flee.

Just like when Sodom burns, you flee.
The flames, they hurt, and you don't wanna feel.
Cuz you're a coward, honey, you have no fight.
So keep meek, keep sweet, and follow.
And should I stray? Like a hole to fill?
Don't, or you'll get cast to the cattle for feed.

But, if you're good, you may feed

that need, darling, more than the want to flee.
What need? I know you like to have that fill.
That's not—I get it: He harms, you feel.
You take the pain as passion, you follow?
Learn to love the lashes, to find flashes from his fight.

But Mama, I don't wanna have his fight.
Well baby, you don't take a He, you can't feed.
Then I'll starve—yeah, and I'll have to follow.
You mean to acquaint me to death while you get to flee?
I'm a worn woman and I don't got hands left to feel.
You get it, hands? Your mama can't even beg bread for a
fill.

We don't have to be whores, Mama. We don't have to have a
fill.
Oh, bless my soul! At my age, and I never thought of that
fight!
You make yourself at the mercy of man, he may feel.
Fake like a sweet stray, and he'll open home and feed.
For us, you get that heart like a honey for his fly to flee.
And when he has you in tradition's white, tradition's
what you'll follow.

Tradition is bride and mother, but what if I don't want to
follow...?
Well, baby, only way to end the line is to refuse to see it
fill.
Well that's easy—I mean to be cast out like Lilith before
you can flee.
Eden's alright, aside from Adam. And you wanna make a
fight?!
You just comply, that's it, and you get to feed.
This life is livable, sweetie, so long as you don't feel.

Maybe I wanna know a sacred battle, a holy fight.
Maybe it's not enough to know where I will feed.
Maybe, Mama, maybe I wanna see how to feel.
Oh, so Miss wants to feel?
On pain or pleasure, from what will you feed?
If you want, baby, take up with life. Throw yourself in, die by first fight.

HEADS UP!

You're going to try a cliché because you feel like shit and maybe public writing might be whimsy enough to pull you out before you really fall in again.

You'll spring for some useless decaf thing because it's 10:32 pm and you feel obligated to pay for this half hour here, but they probably would've preferred if you'd've just taken a table and let them get back to closing.

You'll still get nostalgia for that thrill of the last half hour before clockout at that diner job. You'll still get nausea when you remember the manager that liked to pull your ponytail when you worked BOH.

But let me focus back. Here's what you need to know:

Tomorrow, you're gonna let him kiss you. Nobody's ever taken you out and treated you decently before, so you're always going to be peeking around for the trauma. There's no trauma here. Take your sunglasses off when you get to your car and don't apologize afterwards.

It's going to heat up quick. You haven't gotten anything but that monstrous attention before, so of course you're going to drop as much of the Shy Thing act as you can. You've still *kept ahold of the coin,* atta girl. Spend it when you really catch love. Even if we're climbing up to our 20s now, that has always been the firm vision. And it'll eventually get seen through (?).

I'm starting to think that this particular strain of loneliness is inborn. Like, if that most perfect idea of the afterlife is real and it means that one day everybody gets to strip their souls down and jump into the One, the one we got has some kind of steel shell that only lets us understand the vague idea of warmth from others. Maybe it can be cracked, though. I personally have the fantasy of walking home on a balmy night and suddenly seeing something and *boom,* everything finally connects. But realistically, if we ever hold hands with somebody, I just wanna be able to feel it.

On a related note, numbness is an ongoing problem. You can smile and even make laughs now, but the eyes sometimes don't quite sell it. Start back at practicing faces tonight. Maybe I'll notice some progress here. Not that it's really that big a deal. We both know how the Novocaine Notion has saved us from a spiral time and time again. Pretty soon, you're going to start cataloging little things for when you start getting ignored.

Oh, and you're (probably) going to start getting ignored again. It's been almost 42 hours since the last reply and it's looking like the end. Then again, what did you expect?

It's you, after all.

THE FAT GIRL'S GOOD SCAR

Back home, I would make for the perfect Revolutionary New Diet representative:

> "What on *earth* did you do?!"
> "Don't you just feel so much better now?"
> "Hey, you remember me right? Wow, you look nice…"
> "Damn, I woulda shot my shot in hs if you were like this then."
> "Tan bella, you are much better now."

"You look like a different person."

That, shit, yeah…And I mean like there are a lot of days where I kinda can't really even recognize myself (like it that makes sense?), days where I have to run numbers and grab at everything and put my palms on my new hip bones and put my fingertips on my new collarbone and put my nails on my prospective cheekbones and put my old shorts away and put my hands together for a try at praying and remember that this isn't vanity this is *a cognitive dissonance* and eventually I will be able to connect this person-looking person back to the Old Pictures.

"But you are healthy, right?"

When I hit maintenance (whenever I finally decide that this is maintenance), I think I won't need to center back on the scar. The faint checkmark on my forehead, that is, rather than the lines on my wrists and thighs (it wouldn't be healthy to look at what's on my wrists and thighs). Scars mostly suck because they're for forever, like those teenage lines and the stretches that give away that I didn't always not look like I had some problem, but this one, the forehead one, I'm good with it.

"You don't want any?"

And I think I'm good with it because I have no memory of how it happened. I'm not really even sure what happened (and something had to have happened, ya know, to mark me like that). It's just this innocent thing, free from the other shitty connections. I can start my day by finding it without pulling up those other shitty connections. So cool.

"Sweetie, you should finish that."

That's the constant of my shifting features. So long as I can identify it, see where I'm still kinda the same, I'm alright. Like, I'm okay to go out and be looked at but also not, like, looked at, among the pleasant strangers of this college town and work on myself.

Apparently, I'm working on myself.

SELF-IMPROVEMENT

It's funny how an unseen DM can pull one of those cold creeps through my middle. Literally from almost two years ago, but how can I not come back about the people that hate me? Maybe hate's a strong word—she's right, I *was* a crazy bitch in high school. It's not that "what hurts must be true"; it's the truth, hurt aside. I graduated a dramatic, fat-faced girl going

"ME ME ME"

at every chance to cover over terror. And of course I am so sorry for it, for the way I was and the stories I screamed and all the times I tried flinging my shit onto everybody else, but she was being a normal high-school nasty and I don't know if I've really matured enough to mediate an apology like that. In fact, I know I haven't. So the message (if you can even call it that) will be left without a reply. That, really, is the adult thing to do.

I consider myself *grown* enough now to know I'm maybe even a little underdeveloped for my age. Is my newfound propensity for pigtails because I lost my double chin, or is it unconscious emotional regression? Does my voice really hitch back six years when I'm scared? Who wants to play my shrink? I might just make for the perfect head case, I think.

This almost two-year time-out in Tallahassee has done me some good, though. I've become bearable now. I'm still shocked when people wanna hang out and then hang out *more,* so I see I'm no longer a drainer.

And I'm not a downer, either. Maybe here, right, but I usually keep it *down* and not often *out* and I think it's the Irish in me that's finally bloomed. Or at least the Irish I'm from, the stoics who chose to sink soundless than face the shame of saying they couldn't swim. My old problems are lessened and my new problems look to be lengthy, but I will keep keeping them all under the surface.

Not to say buried, though. I'm going to do it differently than my ancestors. I'll keep my headshit quiet until I have time for making lyrics. Is that a stupid way of putting it, "making lyrics?" The tenet I've been taught for poetry is "putting it fresh," and I've never heard someone say it that way. So I guess I'll say it that way.

And I won't say anything else.

HALLO LONELY

Hi.

How'm I doing?

It's 10:32, this is an empty parking lot, I am a lone young woman, and yet it does as my little safe spot right now.

Safe space—I see it. But I don't...like, I don't really know where else to *be* right now.

So.

Being home always does this to me. I don't get my bubble anymore, not here. I have to...wear flats and have a nice narrative and eat dinner and I can't show my schedule to anybody. Safe space to say, I miss my bubble.

There's too much time in Orlando. At least for me. Everybody else is so busy, busy—I've got hours on hand just to steep in my own bullshit. And y'all know I got a lotta bullshit.

And this is such bullshit too, I know. That teenage thing of getting in your First Car and driving around late, alone, with like Grateful Dead or Chance to croon you through. Hmm. Do people ever outgrow that, though? Like, I wonder if my dad ever does this, or my professors, or the boomers that think that we're all just soft. My cousin grabbed my arm the other day and said I'm all soft, but that's different.

Anyways. Parking lot. Not-too-late night crack at Confessional poetry. I've gone to the gym three days in a row and make my bed every morning.

How'm I doing?

LOOK AT YOU!

I see her well before she sees me—I'm coming up the hill, she's checking her phone—and I already know the eye up-down she's gonna give. I know what she's gonna say. I know what she's gonna ask. I know that later, she's gonna root for every old photo she has and she's gonna send them, one by one, with a "Look at you!" underneath the Before.

Look at me, mm. Looking at me, and looking at Me and Before Me, I can get a little fucked up about it. Contrary to the idea that I forgo food for vanity purposes, I don't like looking at me. I go between seeing hard angles of wrists and clavicles, or the unfortunate trunk of neck and torso. Lately, I've tried to adopt a sort of privileged zen to keep me off my own warring body and away from mirrors.

But I can't avoid texts. And I can't be rude. I always thank them, actually, like another snap of my old self is exactly what I wanted. Like I want to...gloat, I guess. Like since I'm less, I'm better, and I'm so grateful that they see me now. That now they see me. They must've seen me then, though. To have all these candids of me now. To show me all these candids now. To try seeing me candid, now.

I'm being a narcissist now, and that's the point. One must be self-absorbed to truly want to try absorbing the self. And I mean the whole self—like dissipate. Like die. Like don't ever eat Oreos again. Like disappear under the number-drops and look-at-you's till they finally stop.

But right now, her eye's on her phone. My feet are stuck against the incline. Her eyes come off her phone. I can't make myself flee, she's coming fast. I breathe and she's somehow...past, down the road and on her way. I stay. It's still a good day. I guess. The aversion is blessed. But, she saw me—yes?

Or, wow—I really don't seem like myself anymore. My newly-foreign face and my stranger's shape. This girl and I, we grew up together. She's been in my house and I knew all her boyfriends. Shock of unrecognition. No gawking, no oh-my-gods. Just the rush of a campus bus and a knocking in my ribcage that I can't answer.

IIII

CIRCA WHEN I STARTED MOURNING IN RETROSPECT, 2019

SCENES 4 A TROUBLED YOUTH

and 4 E, the girl who loved me when we were 15 (and who'll always be 15)

1: before we'd met I was eleven and almost innocent and in NSB and I

lost a chancla to the chase—
running like a real *rat bitch* against the tongues of the shore.

I'll steal anew off a nice tourist's unattended camp
and give a santy-smile when it's time to sell water.

2: when me and her were so bodily close that some would call too-close

twins, we could tease
(whatever they'll laugh at and let us intake).

And *shh*, because they're almost out of high school, *ok*?
We've always been such cool girls that one won't even
make it out alive (sorry, E****).

3: after E'd up and died and it was such a comfort that

I could get smacked good for a fuck-the-three
but I bite my cheeks hard and bless myself instead.

It's gotten to where I relish in when any She declares me
pure piss in the blood
and I have to act the part. What can I say, baby—I guess
the closet is really my villain's lair.

4: I think I made it and sometimes I feel sorry about it and so

when the month gets too long, I'll just take it by the
quartered week.
In this one, for instance, I may go see a movie. I can
make it to a movie.

That shock of *holy shit you're here?* is finally starting to
mist off a bit.
If I can keep my head straight and up and never peeking
back, I might really make this stick.

****And I swear not speak the Dead's names again.

But E, holy shit, you were crazy, you could spin me out like the breath of God but I could love you in all those other unangelic ways. Did you know where you were going when I came over and cut your hair up into a new girl? When our lips and then our fingers found each other and we tried to call it "for practice?" When your stepbrothers would bang dents into the door and we'd lay like that didn't have our blood scattered? When we had our blood scattered because we knew that they wanted to have us like we had each other? And if you'd had the nerve to put that shit in words, nena, you know I'd have gone without a thought. There was a long time I did think about following after you. And I tried, and I failed, and now I'm a Living Failure.

****And I swear not know the Dead's name again.

HOW I KNOW I'M BAD

You are not a leech,
and I am sorry I ever said otherwise.
I am so sorry that I ever gave you anything
other than absolute affection like you dared
for me.
I'm sorry I loved you
hard, the high school hard of
por siempre You Are Everything
but I would not hold your hand.

Nena, you are all woman
and I'm sorry that I was sorry about loving that,
that I wanted to be a boy so I could have you and
not have
to be a girl that wanted a girl. I'm sorry
that nowadays I'll go Out with a stranger like I'd
never with you.

And nowadays I'm sorry to the memories too, because
sometimes I stay sitting up in the dark and try to

remember how you would sleep with your body open,
facing mine.

UNDERGROWING

is how my grandmother put it when I came and saw her in August. Before August, I hadn't seen her since I'd started it, the undergrowing thing. She decided when she saw me that belts can only do so much and took me to the Macy's warehouse out by Cincinnati. Next day I wore one of the new dresses, this red-and-white striped thing that just hangs on me now. I came downstairs for coffee and she couldn't keep herself from saying *Jesus-Mary&JosephYouHaveGottenSmaller* and I smiled and said thank you the way I've practiced for when people grab at me like that. We went to see my great-grandmother. We all call her Maw. My grandma told me to go up and knock, because I was a surprise visit. Maw opened after a minute and just stared, and she looked almost scared. She had my senior foto on the coffee table. I held it up next to myself and said *now see Maw don't you remember* and I don't know if it really was because of the dementia or what, but she just had to take my word for it that I was really me.

V

CIRCA WHEN I WAS DESPERATELY ALONE AND STARTED HAVING A PROBLEM, LATE 2019–EARLY 2020

DRAMATIC/ON THE END

She tells me while I'm sitting in a Publix parking lot.
I'm here to buy candy for Halloween and to get absolutely fucked up
because it's a one-off sort of night.
It is allowed on holidays and, now,
the news just justifies my misstep even more.

I smile because Mama's always told me she can hear when I do and
hang up on the third *love you baby*.
I'm sitting in my car with the engine off but I end up
at her hospital bed, at the hospital bed that ain't
even happened yet and I'm being silly and dangerous like I'm little
but I don't give a shit, that's my Mama
and she's not supposed to degenerate.
Did I mention that I've got a whore's angel
costume on the whole time?

I stay in the car until I sweat and though the heat prickles my skin

and she can be the cruelest woman I've ever met
this is still the start of an open wound and it festers
like her arms.

NOVEMBER 11TH, 2019

I call home to thank my veteran, but I start seething
how Nam rattled his brain
and everyone warns me that he's not having the best day,
anyway.
I call home and won't give them the real news—I'm
Weight Perfect, the number
they'd wanted from me, because I'll go under in no time
and they're already calling me sick.
I call home because my brother is having his weekly
fifth-life crisis and he needs me to promise
that college isn't so bad but will he please stop talking
about being an astronaut?

I'm coming home in less than two weeks to panic about
a public dinner so it's just
eggs and oatmeal until next Friday. I guess I can blame it
on my paycheck, right? Like, I'm Poor Student and
eating
is sometimes not in the cards. I'm so far
and away from not sleeping on the night bus last year
because I just wanted

to get home and wasn't yet.

HEAVY BABY

I've been reading about girls who drink too much water and it makes their brain swell up and stuff and—

You wanna know if you're gonna die?

Not hoping, just curious.

You're not underweight.

Yet.

Yet, yeah. You are starting to look ***old*** *though, Jesus.*

Smile lines at twenty. Huh. Never knew I smiled enough to make one permanent.

It's probably from deficiencies. Recall in August: your father vaping on a night drive, casual, saying "You don't look good." Then, "I mean, you look thin, but not well." And you don't, you don't look well.

...

But you wanna see thin, don't you?

I just wanna quit seeing where I got extras, I guess.

That's why you're starting to like those man hands. Cupping them bone-peek wrists like you're on your way to some dainty thing. Like that'll absolve you from when you were a woman by twice.

I think they're all being dramatic, though. That's that familial inclination to reach for hysterics. They can't shake *obesity* at me anymore, so now they're really gonna try reaching for a *disorder.*

Or maybe that's what you're trying for.

I think I'm just trying to get out of myself right now. And I can do that much, no?

No?

No?

No?

[ED]DIE K[NO]WS BE[S]T

She brushes her bones up on my big cheeks and whispers the promise of

Ten pounds down to offset Thanksgiving, right?

Of course I know the taste of Oreos, just don't check my kitchen garbage.

Nothing tastes as good as "cuidate mi amor" feels.

Pick and pull and squeeze and then end in a sunrise stretch to call it all Good Morning.

I go through pots of concealer on the monthly now.

I don't get my monthly, now.

The new clothes are starting to fit like the old ones and a belt only goes so far.

Progress is not celebrated, is not shared.

I am twenty years old and a public dinner makes me scared.

sick.

ESTATE OF THE HEIRESS

Again—it apparently takes three generations for a trauma to cycle out. Even grandchildren get touched by those times. I guess I'm just lucky enough to miss out on the Depression.

What'd I get? Aside from a shot of Agent Orange in my bad blood and predisposed to headfuckery? It's not fair for Flint's fall to reach for a Florida girl. You can't ask me to carry Kent State.

Of course, others got the real kind of residue—second-hands I couldn't even name. And, of course, there are people who get trauma direct-delivered. And I guess I got that too. We all do, right? Are y'all walking through the world waiting for a split to set you back?

I hate when people call shit like *demons* and *scars* and *you just keep cycling through all these harming fixes huh.* I call it

Vietnam. I call it Catholicism. I call it the Pacific Theater. I call it Bipolar II, colored cups of brandy, GM shutdown, I call it even the dirty Irish. I call it what he did and what she did after and what I've been doing ever since.

I call it enough.

VI

CIRCA WHEN I GOT BETTER, LATE 2020–EARLY 2021

* * *

Nothing. I wrote nothing.

VII

CIRCA NOW, NOW

THE HIGHLIGHT REEL

I

That delicious
moment when my parents who had always said
you're going to be big as a house and *the world is just not kind to fat girls*
suggested I finish my lunch and
their eyes gave away how terrified they were.

II

The "therapist" or whoever at the Student Center
pointed
out how my nails were naturally purple,
a *serious sign of malnutrition*
and I couldn't stop
admiring them after.

III

I hadn't seen him
in seven weeks and I lost
enough weight
that when he lifted me in his arms I
felt so lovely and light like
I deserved his touch.

IIII

Being sick enough
to lose
consciousness, hair, and my period
and it was finally time I was forced
to call it quits.

V

Being free enough
to finally see
how fucking stupid it all was
and to barely even think about
it now.

TO THE FAT GIRL TERRIFIED AT THE TOP OF A PARKING LOT. (OR, "LIFE LATELY")

The 4th of July is still not a great time
for you and sometimes you drink and invariably you cry
but
it's just one day
and they do say the anniversary is always tough.

You're thin(ish), in love (with a man?!), and paid well (or,
at least, better than you ever thought).
You two—you and your wonderful, emotionally mature,
male partner—are the proud parents
of three black-and-white cats.
Shocker, I know.
You're also retroactively working through all the shit
you were
put through and you still have your moments.

But guess what?
You made it, you really fucking did.
All the things you thought
as you finished what was supposed to be a Last Milk-
shake and

stared down at the impact below—
they weren't that big of a deal after all.

That is not to say you were ever just a drama queen,
and you shouldn't ever let *anyone* write you off like that again.
You were suffering, even if nobody else saw that.
And even though you decided to survive, you
still had to suffer more before the real breakthrough.

It's been four years and now you only get
flashes of what you felt then.
They hurt, I won't bullshit you.
But what you have now—
who you clawed your way to becoming—
I swear, it was fucking worth it.

It is fucking worth it.

NOTE ON PAGE 1 OF MY FINAL PROJECT FOR PROFESSOR TANYA GRAE'S CLASS.

I'd tentatively like to call this collection of poems "Body Spells."

ACKNOWLEDGMENTS

Thank you to my family: Gramma, Papa, Dad, Mona, Aunt Meg, Mom, Gabby, Max, and everyone else.

Thank you to my friends: Priscilla, Angela, Iman, and Melisa especially.

And thank you, Camren. You were what made me want to recover and build the life we have today. I love you.

ABOUT THE AUTHOR

Zero is the pen name of a 20-something in Orlando, Florida.

ALSO BY ZERO

WHO MOTHERED THE CORPSE?

Who mothered the
corpse?

a novella by Zero

She is found by a hunter one Sunday morning.

She lays, as though asleep, on the forest floor.

She has no name, but she had four mothers.

In a world where the dead are used without qualms by the living, the body of a beautiful young girl is claimed by four women: a witch, an artist, a whore, and a chef. Each allege to be her mother, and each have their own posthumous plans for her. Which woman will get to fulfill her desires? Who mothered the corpse? With the true possessor in question, a trial commences.

Available on Amazon.

SHE'LL GET THERE: STORIES THAT NO LONGER HURT.

In this story collection, the reader encounters four women—Clara, Marta, Georgia, and Lala—with difficult pasts and uncertain futures. Faced with real-life bogeymen, death, and unrequited loves, each woman must reckon with what has been done and choose what will happen to her. Zero's debut story collection weaves together real-life experiences to create a complex portrait of victims, witnesses, survivors, and aggressors alike.

Available on Amazon.

REQUEST FOR THE READER

If you liked this book, please leave an honest review on my Amazon page. It is tremendously helpful in boosting my visibility to others. Thank you.

www.ingramcontent.com/pod-product-compliance
Lightning Source LLC
LaVergne TN
LVHW012113160826
845678LV00014B/3070

* 9 7 9 8 3 6 7 1 4 0 1 5 6 *